Contents

Introduction	3
Program Components	4
Why Use Learning Centers?	6
Correlation to the National Science Education Standards (by Standard)	8
Correlation to the National Science Education Standards (by Activity)	9
What Is Science?	12
Using Learning Centers	14
Planning the Room	14
Classroom Setup 1	15
Classroom Setup 2	16
Your Own Classroom Setup	17
Scheduling Centers Time and Setting Up	18
Preparing the Students	19
Establishing Student Pairs	19
Students with Special Needs	19
Promoting Safety	20
Setting and Modeling Expectations for Behavior	21
Reinforcing Rules of Behavior	22
Traffic Flow and Transitions	23
Setting Up a Rotation Plan	24
Introducing Centers Activities	26
Sample Introductory Week	27
Cleaning Up and Storing Materials	31
Assessing and Evaluating Learning	32
Informal Assessment	33
Anecdotal Records	34
Student Work	35
Student Self-Evaluation	36
Family and Community Involvement	37
Wish List	39
References	40
Blackline Masters	41

Introduction

Your ticket to success! **CenterStage SCIENCE**

Welcome to CenterStage Science™ learning centers. This program is designed to help your students learn more about science as they participate in science processes, such as observing, predicting, and classifying. Students can benefit from its engaging activities throughout the school year.

There are three CenterStage Science centers at each grade level: Physical Science, Life Science, and Earth Science. Activities for each center address one or more science content standards as presented in the *National Science Education Standards* [National Research Council, 1996].

Use CenterStage Science learning centers to foster student independence while providing opportunities for hands-on, minds-on work with science.

Complete, ready-to-use CenterStage Science learning centers provide you with

- ★ engaging, ready-to-use Activity Cards and science tools, specimens, books, and other materials
- ★ easy-to-use teaching notes
- ★ blackline masters to provide additional information and facilitate recording results

CenterStage Science learning centers enable you to

- ★ maximize and diversify instructional time, since many CenterStage Science activities can fit effectively into literacy block time
- ★ work directly with individuals and small groups while others are engaged in center work
- ★ target individual needs and interests
- ★ develop student skill in using science processes and tools
- ★ assess student progress
- ★ reinforce reading and math skills that are inherent in doing science
- ★ help students appreciate the richness of science while enjoying the excitement and satisfaction that come with discovery

Even if you have never used centers before, this program is for you! You will learn how to

- ★ set up learning centers in your classroom
- ★ introduce center-based activities
- ★ manage your classroom for work in centers
- ★ help each student become a responsible, independent learner

CenterStage Science activities can fit into literacy block time.

- ★ Many activities are literacy based.
- ★ Activities require reading, thinking, and speaking.
- ★ Activities include a writing prompt.
- ★ Activities encourage vocabulary development.

CenterStage™ Science Learning Centers   Teacher's Resource Guide   3

CenterStage™ Science Makes It Easy to Use A Center-Based Approach!

Activity Cards promote engaging, hands-on exploration and are laminated for durability.

CenterStage Science Grade 3 Physical Science Center shown here.

18 Activity Cards in Each Center!

- Easy-to-follow directions show the appropriate materials to use.
- Open-ended, exploratory activities with hands-on opportunities increase understanding of challenging topics.
- Writing prompts encourage students to explain their thinking.

Teacher's Resource Guide   CenterStage™ Science Learning Centers

CenterStage SCIENCE

Storage carrel unfolds to create a self-contained work area.

Books and materials used in each activity come organized in seven detachable storage pouches.

Teacher's Notes offer practical management and record-keeping tools for each activity, including assessment guidelines and both content and process objectives.

Teacher's Resource Guide provides comprehensive support, including correlations to standards, a scope and sequence, and classroom management suggestions.

CenterStage Science is Easy to Use!

1. Select a center. 
2. Open the storage carrel. 
3. Set out an activity.

CenterStage™ Science Learning Centers — Teacher's Resource Guide

Why Use Learning Centers?

Learning centers provide students with an opportunity to work at their own pace in ways that complement their individual learning styles. The Activity Cards for each center address visual, auditory, and kinesthetic learners. Students will enjoy the appealing cards, which contain easy-to-follow directions and colorful graphics that support concepts, skills, and processes.

Students are encouraged to talk about their investigations through specific prompts in the directions. As they share their ideas, they will elaborate upon individual ideas, enhance their conceptual understanding, and add to their scientific vocabulary. The learning centers in each module are designed to help students integrate science process skills, such as observation, communication, using mathematics, and using time and spatial relationships, with conceptual understanding.

Learning center activities may be used to provide valuable and exciting opportunities for students to supplement the material being studied in class, or to investigate topics of special interest to them.

Eric Jensen [1998] has suggested that students become motivated learners when assignments are engaging, personally relevant, and tailored to individual needs. Jensen also suggested that a simple change in location helps get the brain's attention, while providing a balance of predictable and novel assignments helps energize the brain.

These are the factors that make CenterStage Science effective and exciting teaching and learning tools.

- When you set up CenterStage Science learning centers, you invite students to move to different places in the classroom.
- When you introduce a new activity, you invite students to engage in learning and build on what they already know.
- The mix of activities and games in CenterStage Science provides a variety of contexts for learning and practicing skills individually or with a partner.

Carol Ann Tomlinson [2002] summarized how well-designed stations (centers) help teachers meet the needs of individual students. Stations should

- focus on important learning goals
- include activities that vary from simple to complex
- allow different students to work on different tasks
- invite flexible grouping
- lend themselves to a good balance of teacher choice and student choice

When you use CenterStage Science learning centers in your classroom, you give students experience in directing and taking responsibility for their own learning. Learning becomes more student centered and less teacher directed. The real-life skills that are acquired through the use of learning centers—cooperation, time management, independence, flexibility, and responsibility, among others—are the critical skills that students need as they construct a deep and long-lasting understanding of science and as they gradually enter the adult world.

Learning centers can help you meet the challenges of today's classrooms: finding time to work with individuals or small groups of students to meet their individual needs, ensuring appropriate concept development and practice for students, and managing a diverse classroom. The top seven reasons to use CenterStage Science learning centers in your classroom are listed here:

1. Learning centers provide an engaging way to explore, practice, or review key science concepts and skills.
2. Learning centers motivate students to review and practice key concepts and science processes and master key skills.
3. Learning centers free teachers to interact with students in small groups.
4. Learning centers enable teachers to better understand the needs of individual students in a small group while other students are engaged in worthwhile learning center activities.
5. Learning centers provide an opportunity for students to become more independent learners who try new strategies and explore new concepts.
6. Learning centers can present problem-solving opportunities that encourage students to try out challenging tasks in a low-risk environment.
7. Learning centers can help you create a social environment that allows students to interact and collaborate with peers.

Correlation to the National Science Education Standards (by Standard)

	Grade 1	Grade 2	Grade 3
Underlying Concepts and Processes			
Systems, order, and organization	○	○	○
Evidence, models, and explanation	○	○	○
Change, constancy, and measurement	○	○	○
Evolution and Equilibrium			
Form and Function	○	○	○
Science as Inquiry			
Abilities necessary to do scientific inquiry	○	○	○
Understanding about scientific inquiry	○	○	○
Physical Science			
Properties of objects and materials	○	○	○
Position and motion of objects	○	○	○
Light, heat, electricity, and magnetism	○	○	○
Life Science			
Characteristics of organisms	○	○	○
Life cycles of organisms	○	○	○
Organisms and environments	○	○	○
Earth and Space Science			
Properties of earth materials	○	○	○
Objects in the sky	○	○	○
Changes in earth and sky	○	○	○
Science and Technology			
Abilities of technological design	○	○	○
Understanding about science and technology	○	○	○
Abilities to distinguish between natural objects and objects made by humans	○	○	
Science in Personal and Social Perspectives			
Personal health	○		○
Characteristics and changes in population	○	○	○
Types of resources	○	○	○
Changes in environments	○	○	○
Science and technology in local challenges	○	○	○
History and Nature of Science			
Science as a human endeavor	○	○	○

Correlation to the National Science Education Standards (by Activity)

	Grade 1	Grade 2	Grade 3
Physical Science			
Properties of objects and materials	1, 2, 3, 4, 5, 6, 9, 11	1, 2, 3, 4, 7, 14, 18	1, 2, 3, 5, 6, 7, 18
Position and motion of objects	2, 5, 6, 7, 8, 18	4, 5, 6, 8	4, 6, 7, 8, 9, 10, 11, 17
Light, heat, electricity, and magnetism	10, 12, 13, 14, 15, 16, 17	9, 10, 11, 12, 13, 14, 15, 16, 17	3, 12, 13, 14, 15, 16
Life Science			
Characteristics of organisms	1, 2, 3, 4, 5, 6, 7, 8, 9, 10, 11, 12, 14, 16	1, 2, 4, 5, 6, 7, 8, 9, 10, 11, 12, 13, 14, 18	1, 2, 5, 8, 9, 10, 11, 12, 15, 16, 17
Life cycles of organisms	13, 15	3, 9	1, 3, 11
Organisms and environments	2, 9, 16, 17, 18	4, 12, 15, 16, 17, 18	3, 4, 6, 7, 13, 14, 18
Earth and Space Science			
Properties of earth materials	1, 2, 3, 4, 5, 6, 7, 8, 9, 10, 11	1, 2, 3, 4, 6, 7, 8, 9, 10, 12	1, 2, 3, 4, 5, 6, 7, 9, 10, 11
Objects in the sky	12, 13, 14, 15, 16, 17, 18	13, 14, 15, 16, 17, 18	12, 13, 16, 17, 18
Changes in earth and sky	6, 12, 14, 15	5, 6, 11, 12, 13, 15	6, 7, 8, 14, 15, 17

Your ticket to success!

Center Stage
SCIENCE

What Is Science?

Science is not a collection of facts to be memorized or a step-by-step procedure for which the end result is already known. Science is the thoughtful process of collecting and organizing facts and making observations in order to discover meaningful patterns and, ultimately, to make predictions. Information from scientific investigations can be represented in many different ways. Depending on the nature of the observations and the purpose of the investigation, scientists may use drawings, tables and charts, bar and line graphs, and so forth to help them make sense of the information collected. Through the science processes of observing, classifying, predicting, asking questions, communicating, using mathematics, making hypotheses, controlling and manipulating variables, and using time and spatial relationships, new information and insights may be integrated with prior knowledge to create a deeper and more realistic picture of the natural world and how it works.

Science is ever changing and self-correcting. Scientists constantly check the predictions of existing models against what they observe in the real world in order to determine how well the existing scientific schema function. Because science is based on the free exchange of information and ideas, once an experiment or a series of observations is described and published, it is subject to vigorous scrutiny. Through this process, ideas are tested and then refined, corrected, or even abandoned. This ongoing process helps to ensure progress toward a more accurate and complete description of the natural world. As new testing procedures and instruments with increasing sensitivity are developed, scientific knowledge will continue to grow and evolve. In the elementary classroom, teachers must provide opportunities for students to realize that "although men and women using scientific inquiry have learned much about objects, events, and phenomena in nature, much more remains to be understood" and that "science will never be finished" [National Research Council, 1996].

Scientific investigations take three basic forms: descriptive, classificatory, and explanatory. The descriptive science investigation entails making careful observations about an object's characteristics or properties. In a study of plants, for example, students might describe the shape, color, size, or texture of their different seeds. In the classificatory investigation, students might put the seeds in different groups based on similar characteristics. Seeds that are large, smooth, oblong, and white might be classified as white lima beans. In the explanatory investigation, students might design an experiment to determine the effect of different amounts of fertilizer on the growth of corn plants.

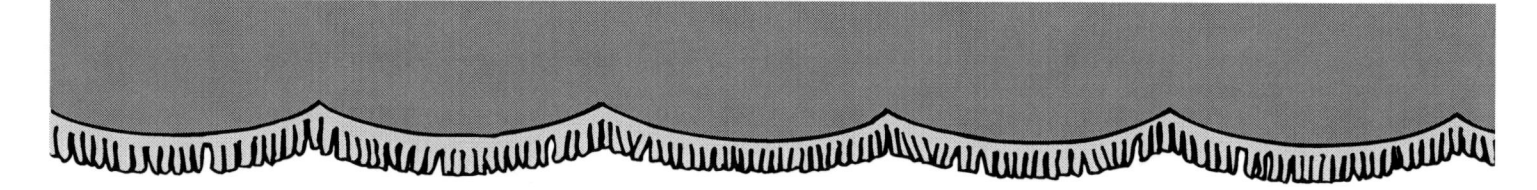

Science understanding typically incorporates content, processes, and attitudes. Understanding is a central goal of science education. Researchers suggest that when students understand, they are able to connect new knowledge to prior knowledge, interpret what they learn, apply knowledge to new situations, and explain and predict phenomena and events. [Wiggins and McTigue, 1998; Wiske, 1998]. Through the CenterStage Science learning activities, teachers are able to guide students to interpret, apply knowledge, explain, and make new connections as well as "encourage and model the skills of scientific inquiry" [National Research Council, 1996]. In order for students to close the gap between their own understanding and the accepted conventions of the scientific community, teachers must focus on student understanding and use of scientific knowledge and process skills and promote open-mindedness.

Science investigations tap into a child's natural curiosity and sense of wonder. Through CenterStage Science learning activities, students will work to develop deep and long-lasting understandings of the natural world, enhance their scientific vocabulary, extend their ability to collect and represent their findings, and refine their ability to discuss and examine their own ideas. In connecting science with mathematics, reading, and writing, students and their teachers will better appreciate the interconnectedness of all content areas.

Using Learning Centers

"Teachers of science design and manage learning environments that provide students with the time, space, and resources needed for learning science." [*NSES*, p. 43]

Planning the Room

Your ticket to success!
CenterStage SCIENCE

Learning centers can be set up in any of several different ways. Choose a setup that is compatible with your teaching style and available classroom space. Here are some ideas:

Step 1: Make a sketch of your classroom on graph paper. Note all windows, doors, desks, outlets, and display areas.

Step 2: Plan areas where centers will be displayed and used. Be sure students can move to, from, and between centers without disturbing others.

Ideally, each CenterStage Science learning center is set up as a stationary, carrel-style work station that is large enough to accommodate the center itself, the materials, and one or two students. Position the learning center table against a wall or next to a bulletin board or bookcase. Post the center rules on the wall or bottom section of the bulletin board. If space is limited, you can set up a "mobile center" that students visit to get an Activity Card and the necessary materials, and then move to another area of the classroom to work.

Keep these things in mind as you plan the placement of your learning centers.

1. **Permanent Fixtures.** Consider the locations of all electrical outlets, bulletin boards, windows, and other fixtures. Avoid placing learning centers in front of windows or behind doors that are used regularly.

2. **Traffic Flow.** Arrange the learning centers so that there is enough room for students to move from one classroom area to another without disturbing others. Establish pathways for students to use during center time.

3. **Quiet and Noisy Areas.** Position centers away from areas where other students may need quiet to focus on other tasks.

4. **Well-Lighted Areas.** Since many CenterStage Science activities require keen observation, reading, and writing, arrange to have adequate lighting over the center area. The activities themselves do not require an electrical outlet.

Try one of the classroom setups shown on the next two pages, or use the grid provided to design the best arrangement for your classroom.

Classroom Setup 1

"My students and I work best when their desks are organized in rows. I want to set up centers so pairs of students can pick up materials and take them back to their seats."

This floor plan shows three different center placement options. Placement 1 allows for good traffic flow. Also, the nearby bulletin board and display area is a convenient place to set up any related or enrichment materials, or even a file where students can place their finished work. Placement 2 is far from the door and teacher's desk. Students can reach the center by walking behind their classmates' desks. The bulletin board and display area can be used to display and file completed work. Placement 3, to the side of the room, may be the least disruptive for students who are easily distracted. Students might file work in a box or folder on top of the bookshelves.

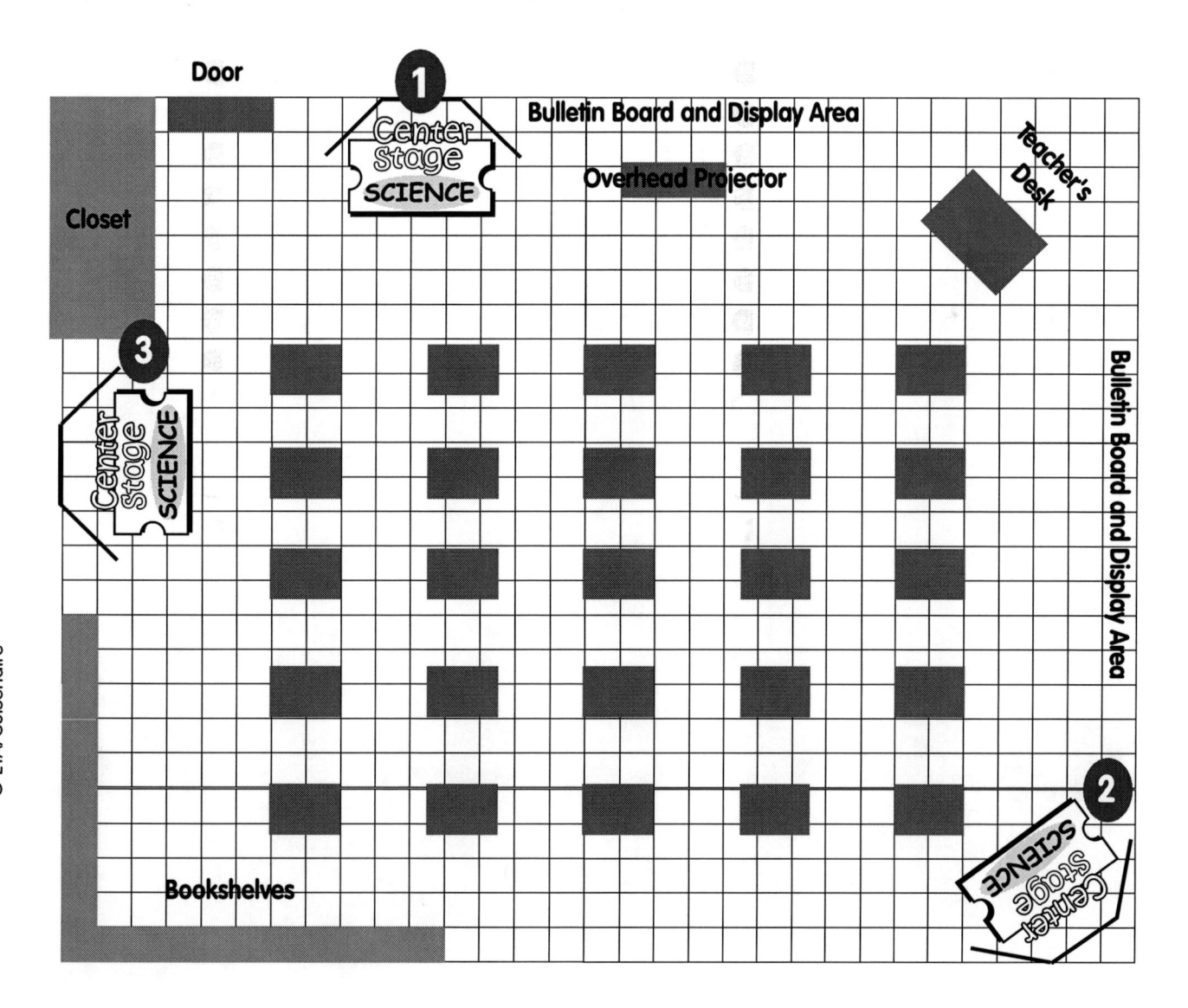

CenterStage™ Science Learning Centers — Teacher's Resource Guide

Classroom Setup 2

"My students sit at tables of four. I want pairs to be able to move to a learning center to do activities. That way, students can work with appropriate partners and support each other at center time."

This floor plan shows three possible locations for CenterStage Science centers. Some or all of the centers could be used simultaneously. Center 2, placed near the conference area and teacher's desk, can be used by students who may need more monitoring and direction as they work. Student papers may be displayed and filed near each center.

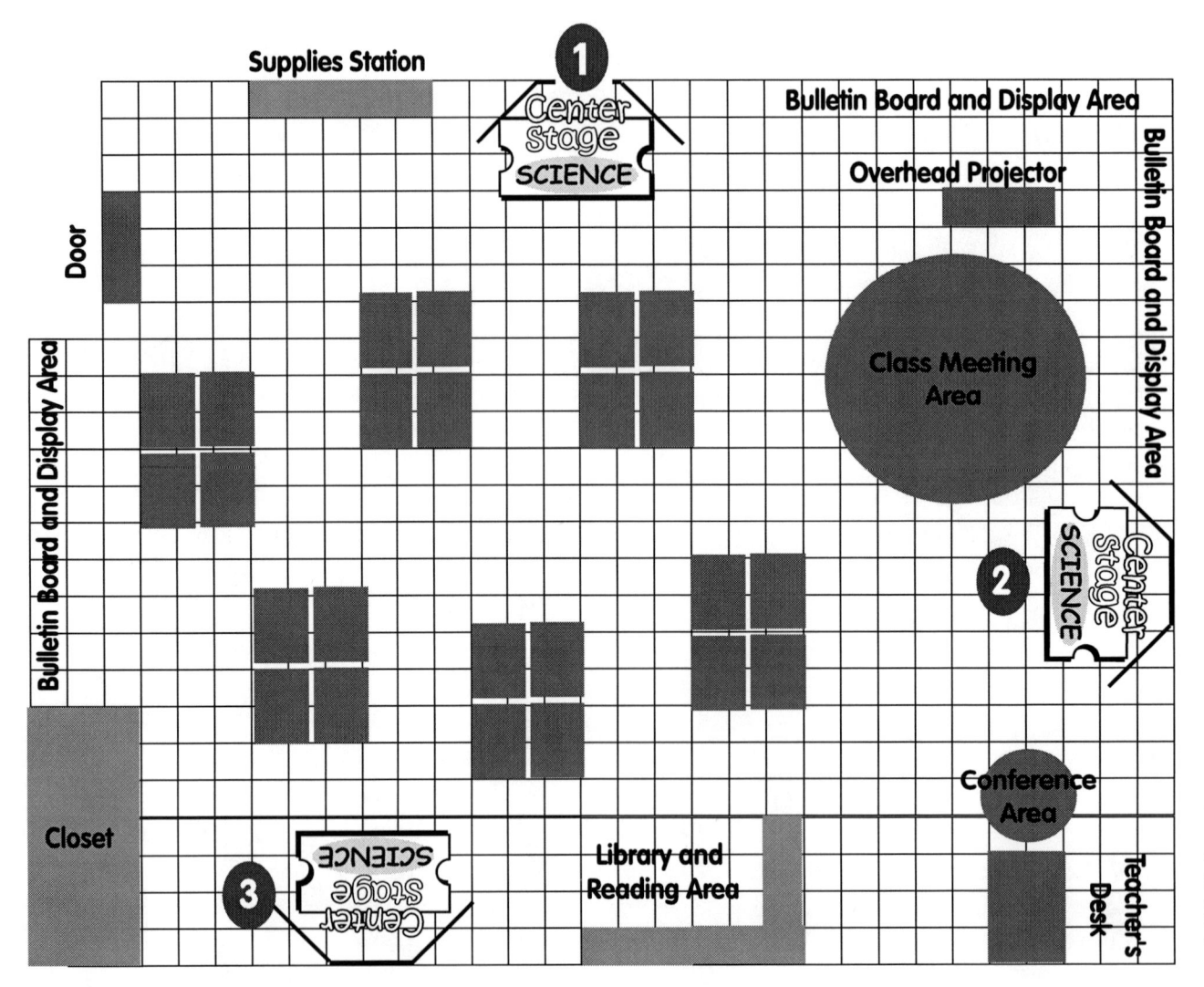

Your Own Classroom Setup

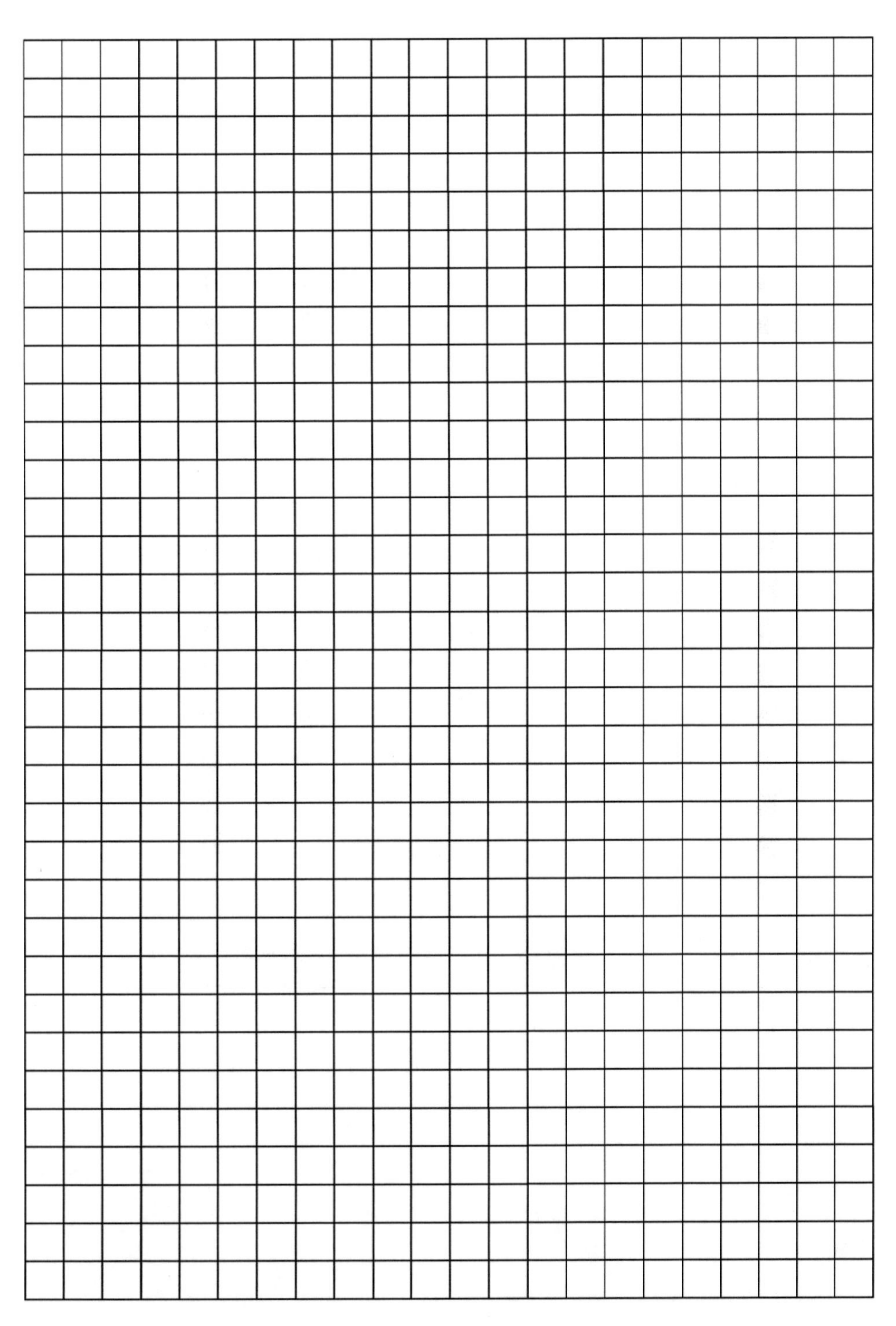

Draw a floor plan of your classroom. Locate and sketch in the following:

- Doors
- Windows
- Outlets
- Overhead projector
- Bulletin boards
- Shelves
- Other fixed areas
- Teacher's desk
- Student desks

Then decide where to set up your CenterStage Science learning centers.

Scheduling Centers Time and Setting Up

Your ticket to success! **CenterStage SCIENCE**

Careful planning is the key to successful teaching. Before you can begin using centers, you will need to decide the following:

1. How often will you use centers?

2. How many centers do you want to set up at one time?

3. Do you want all students to be working on the same topic, or do you want different centers to address different topics or subjects?

Start by having Centers Day once a week. The day can be the focal point of the week, and it may even motivate students to complete other assignments. Centers Day can provide a refreshing break from routine instruction for everyone.

Schedule 60–90 minutes on an afternoon late in the week. Students can take 20-minute turns at one of several open centers while classmates pursue free reading, quiet educational games, or other student-directed activities. Once routines for center work are established, you might use this time to work with students who need extra help—or you might circulate and make notes about student interests and progress.

You may prefer to open centers at specific times several days a week—during seat work time, when you work with small groups while the rest of the class is engaged in reading, during pull-out programs, before all students have arrived in the morning, during indoor recess, or after school for students who stay late or wait for late buses.

If your class is new to centers, it's a good idea to open centers one at a time, emphasizing appropriate behavior and use of equipment, and debriefing students afterward. During this time you can encourage students to suggest ways to help things run more smoothly the next time they use centers.

Experienced teachers suggest utilizing no more than three or four learning centers at any given time. The centers may all be CenterStage Science, or they may be centers for other subject areas—perhaps reading, writing, or math. (See CenterStage Math at www.etacuisenaire.com.)

CenterStage Science centers are easy to set up. You simply unfold the module to form a carrel on a tabletop. Then choose an Activity Card and select the necessary materials from their storage pouches. Before using any module, check the Teacher's Notes for any classroom materials (ruler, paper clip) or local materials students will need to complete the activity. The notes will also suggest materials you may add to enrich the activities (local rocks, pictures, books from your classroom or school library, and so forth).

Once students are used to working in CenterStage Science centers, you might select a small team of students who will change the Activity Cards and set out needed materials from the module. These students can also be sure materials are cleaned up and put away when the class is finished with the center.

Preparing the Students

Your ticket to success! **CenterStage SCIENCE**

"Set up learning groups and encourage students to work together to investigate science questions and topics." [Chessin and Shaw, 2002]

Establishing Student Pairs

Most CenterStage Science activities are designed to be used by pairs of students. You may already have effective techniques for establishing student partners, but if not, consider grouping students according to the following:

- Students with about the same levels of ability and motivation
- Students who are friends (If you allow students to choose their own partners, be sure no one is left out.)
- A student who is a good reader with a less-able reader
- Students with similar personalities, behaviors, or interests (two shy students, two enthusiastic students, two students who are particularly interested in dinosaurs)
- A student who is learning English and a proficient English speaker
- Students may be assigned partners at random

Once partners are established, you may wish to maintain those partnerships for a period of time—a grading period or a semester. This will result in less confusion, less time spent "getting to know you," and therefore more time for productive work.

For very cooperative children who can share materials and responsibilities, you may wish to place the students in groups of three.

Students with Special Needs

"Recognize and respond to student diversity and encourage all students to participate fully in science learning." [*NSES*, p. 32]

Partner work and small-group learning frequently offer a more favorable environment for special needs students than whole-class instruction. Learning centers can provide such a favorable environment.

As a group, the games and activities in CenterStage Science have multiple entry points and engage students in multiple modalities. Students with special needs can participate in these activities in ways that address how they learn new material best.

The behavioral management strategies described in this guide will benefit special needs students as well. Notice how these management strategies help students visualize routines, anticipate next steps, monitor their own behaviors, and engage in activities in multiple modalities.

Some students may require additional accommodation. Many of your existing strategies for inclusion will work just as well with centers as they do in the regular classroom:

- Auditory, visual, and kinesthetic support
- Proximity support
- Peer-learning and support
- Specialized work spaces

For example, for students who do not work successfully even in small groups, you can provide alternatives. Students may

- participate while sitting near the teacher (proximity support)
- work with an older student or an adult partner (peer-learning and support)
- do the activity as an individual at a separate desk (specialized work space)

If your classroom includes special needs students for whom any loosely structured learning environment is too challenging, consult with the Resource Specialist or the Special Education Coordinator in your district. Share your centers plan with him or her and ask for help in tailoring CenterStage Science activities to the needs of specific students.

It is impossible to anticipate which strategies will be effective in any specific case. In many cases, a combination of strategies leads to success. Be flexible. If one strategy doesn't help the student participate in the learning experience, try another. Continue to express your confidence in each student, affirming that he or she is a capable learner.

Promoting Safety

Teachers must be aware of safety precautions and regulations whenever students are engaged in science investigations. It is important to review and post safety rules so that students are aware of them. Although the activities in CenterStage Science are designed to be completed without safety goggles, if wearing goggles is standard procedure in your classroom, have students wear them while working in science centers. A variety of safety goggles and glasses are available from ETA/Cuisenaire. All protective eyewear meets ANSI Z87.1 standards.

Some general safety guidelines for students are as follows. (A blackline master is provided for you in the Blackline Masters section of this *Guide*.)

- Do not taste, eat, or drink any materials.
- Wash your hands after handling messy materials.
- Report any accidents.
- Tell your teacher if you have allergies or other medical problems.
- Wear safety goggles.

Setting and Modeling Expectations for Behavior

"Challenge students to accept and share responsibility for their own learning ... individually and as members of a group." [*NSES*, p. 36]

Your leadership and consistent reinforcement of appropriate behaviors are important keys to your students' success. Students want to follow the rules and are most successful in doing so when they have participated in setting them. If you already have developed and posted rules of behavior in your classroom, lead a discussion that guides students in applying those rules to their work in centers.

If you do not already have rules in place, you might want to use or adapt the one supplied. (A blackline master is provided in the Blackline Masters section of this *Guide*.)

Display **Rules for Learning Centers.**

Read the first rule aloud. (Respect yourself and others.)

Ask: What does respect look like when we use our learning centers? What are some ways we can show respect to ourselves and to our classmates?

Give students time to visualize respectful behavior. Then invite students to offer examples. These will be statements such as

> I walk quietly from my seat to the center.
>
> We help each other during the activity.
>
> We take turns discussing things and doing the writing.

Ask: What does respect sound like during center time?

Ask for volunteers. Some possible responses are

> We talk in quiet voices
>
> We ask, "What are your ideas?" or "What do you think?"
>
> We say, "What can we add to the drawing?"
>
> We say, "Share the colored pencils with me, please."

Discuss each rule in turn. You may also want to discuss some of the following responses and ask students to match the behavior to one or more of the rules.

What does respect *look* like?	What does respect *sound* like?
Be friendly and polite.	"Please."
Keep your hands and feet to yourself.	"Use your partner voice."
Walk and sit quietly and calmly.	"I didn't understand that. Please read it again."
Use quiet voices.	"Thank you."
Wait until your partner is finished speaking before you share your ideas.	"Please hand me the magnifier."

CenterStage™ Science Learning Centers   Teacher's Resource Guide

What does respect *look* like?	What does respect *sound* like?
Check under the tables and chairs. Put materials back.	"May I have my turn now?"
Review the whole card. Then start work.	"Time's about up. Let's clean up."
Share the specimens and tools.	"Whose turn is it to write now?"

Reinforcing Rules of Behavior

We need increased emphasis on "supporting a classroom with cooperation, shared responsibility, and respect." [*NSES*, p. 52]

Whenever you address rules of behavior, be specific. Always reinforce rules by stating a positive behavior—something that the student *can* do. Express confidence that students are able to learn positive classroom behaviors.

Instead of saying "Don't run!"
   Do say, "Please walk in the classroom. Go back to your seat and try again. Walk to the center."

Instead of saying "Don't bother your partner."
   Do say, "Please keep your hands on your part of the table (in your lap, in front of you). I know you can remember to respect yourself and your partner."

Instead of saying "Don't be so loud!"
   Do say, "Please use your partner voice. I know you want a quiet classroom where everyone can hear and work."

When you clearly state the behavior you *do* want to see and consistently reinforce positive behaviors with verbal clues, students are better able to internalize and exhibit the desired behaviors.

When everyone has had a chance to work at the center, debrief students by discussing the experience with them. Focus on what they learned and also on the behaviors that helped make the experience positive and successful.

Remember

- After you set expectations for behavior, reinforce them by stating positive behaviors.
- Guide students as they work, making comments that reinforce desired behaviors.
- Debrief students afterward, focusing on what they learned and on the behaviors that helped make learning possible.

Traffic Flow and Transitions

Effectively managing student traffic helps any classroom run more smoothly. You undoubtedly have routines for the various transitions that occur during the day: beginning and ending the day, moving into and out of the classroom, and going to and returning from recess and lunch.

When you use centers in the classroom, you will want to use one or more of those routines to help students assume responsibility for getting to and from centers in an orderly way. Here are some further suggestions:

1. Post a list of students who will be working in centers that day. Be sure to place it where students can check it easily. Lists could be displayed on the writing board or bulletin board.

2. Clearly signal transition times and help students practice good transition behaviors. Select a statement, sound, or visual signal (announce the center time, ring a bell, flash the lights off and on) that tells students they may go to centers. Be sure that students recognize the signal and know that it means that they should finish up their current activity and move to their assigned centers.

3. Remember that CenterStage Science modules are designed to help students work through the investigations competently and develop learning independence. Because each investigation is designed to take a given amount of time (approximately 20 minutes, not including the Learn More, which may require a longer time commitment for research or writing), students are responsible for keeping track of time and working both efficiently and effectively.

Model how to use a VersaTimer (or a clock or watch with a second hand) with your students so that they are able to monitor their pace and make adjustments as necessary. After you set clear expectations for keeping time and cleaning up, remind students of behaviors that will allow them to make the best use of their time and that will make their experience positive and successful.

Setting Up a Rotation Plan

When student pairs have been established and the procedures for moving around the classroom are clear, post a rotation plan on the bulletin board. Entries will include the names of the student pairs and the days they will be using the centers.

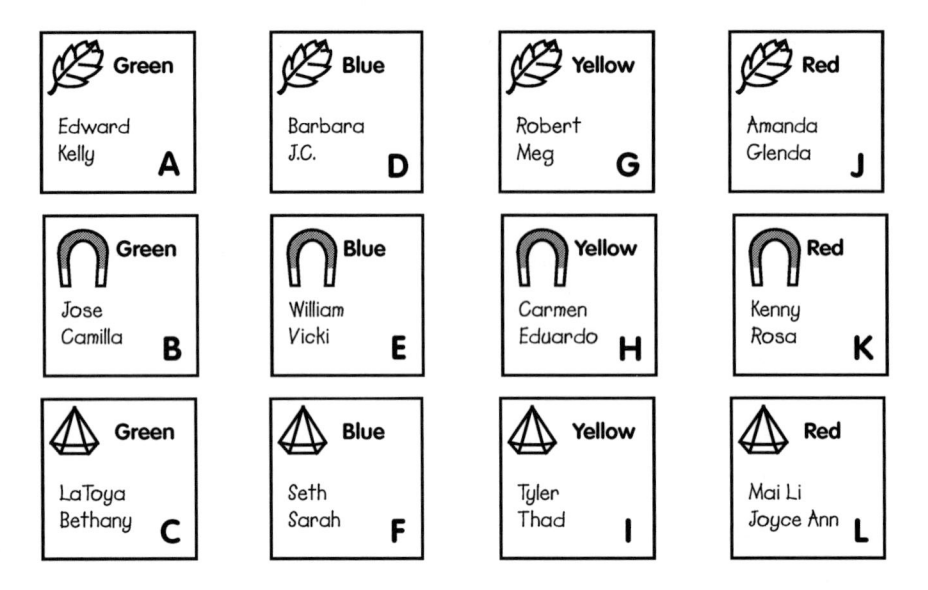

Green — Edward, Kelly **A**	Blue — Barbara, J.C. **D**	Yellow — Robert, Meg **G**	Red — Amanda, Glenda **J**
Green — Jose, Camilla **B**	Blue — William, Vicki **E**	Yellow — Carmen, Eduardo **H**	Red — Kenny, Rosa **K**
Green — LaToya, Bethany **C**	Blue — Seth, Sarah **F**	Yellow — Tyler, Thad **I**	Red — Mai Li, Joyce Ann **L**

Centers Rotation Chart 1

Session 1		CSS Center 1	CSS Center 2	CSS Center 3	Small Group with Teacher	Independent Reading	Games
Center Time	20	A	B	C	D, E, F	G, H, I	J, K, L
Transition	5						
Center Time	20	J	K	L	A, B, C	D, E, F	G, H, I
Transition	5						
Center Time	20	G	H	I	J, K, L	A, B, C	D, E, F
Transition	5						
Center Time	20	D	E	F	G, H, I	J, K, L	A, B, C
Transition	5						

Centers Rotation Chart 2

Session 2			CSS Center 1	CSS Center 2	CSS Center 3	Small Group with Teacher	Independent Reading	Games
Center Time	20		C	A	B	D, E, F	G, H, I	J, K, L
Transition	5							
Center Time	20		L	J	K	A, B, C	D, E, F	G, H, I
Transition	5							
Center Time	20		I	G	H	J, K, L	A, B, C	D, E, F
Transition	5							
Center Time	20		F	D	E	G, H, I	J, K, L	A, B, C
Transition	5							

Centers Rotation Chart 3

Session 3			CSS Center 1	CSS Center 2	CSS Center 3	Small Group with Teacher	Independent Reading	Games
Center Time	20		B	C	A	D, E, F	G, H, I	J, K, L
Transition	5							
Center Time	20		K	L	J	A, B, C	D, E, F	G, H, I
Transition	5							
Center Time	20		H	I	G	J, K, L	A, B, C	D, E, F
Transition	5							
Center Time	20		E	F	D	G, H, I	J, K, L	A, B, C
Transition	5							

Introducing Centers Activities

Checklist

☐ You have decided where to set up centers in your classroom.
☐ You have established expectations for behavior, for clean up, and/or for leaving the center ready for the next group.
☐ You have anticipated travel time and traffic patterns.
☐ You have decided what to focus on in each center.
☐ You have established student pairs and set up a rotation plan for them to follow.

Now you are ready to introduce students to the activities themselves. Remember that the time you spend introducing centers is time well spent. Students that are properly prepared will benefit the most from their experiences.

Introductory Week Overview

(See next section for more detail.)

Days 1, 2, and 3

Allow about 15 minutes for each of three days in a row. Each day introduce the class to one center you will use during the week. Model the activity for students.

Day 4

Set aside about 20–30 minutes for students to observe a pair of students at each center talking through the steps for completing an activity. Have the rest of the class gather around and note those behaviors that are helpful and those that need to be improved in order to make the center more successful.

Day 5

Review the activities that are available to students in the centers. Remind them of appropriate center behavior.

Allow 60–90 minutes for work in Centers. Debrief students afterward: What did they learn? What behaviors allowed things to work more smoothly? What could be changed to make center time even better?

> **Remember**
>
> Centers will be more successful if you keep the following in mind:
>
> - Make sure students understand the activity they will be working on and know what to do in order to complete it successfully
> - Set out materials for easy student use
> - Emphasize safety and the appropriate use of tools and specimens
> - Explain procedures for cleaning up materials after their use
> - Establish a routine for keeping records and handing in work
> - Clearly outline guidelines for expected behavior
> - Maintain predictable routines for moving to and from centers
> - Debrief students from time to time to check their understanding and to reinforce desired behaviors and procedures
> - Provide all students with an opportunity to work at centers

Sample Introductory Week

Suggestions for the first week you use centers are provided here. After that, students will become more accustomed to working in centers, and you will not have to spend as much time monitoring the routines.

Review the Teacher Notes for the activity you plan to introduce. The notes will suggest ways to prepare students for the activity. Try the activity on your own, taking notes and making refinements as necessary to fit your purposes and the knowledge and abilities of your class. Decide whether you want students to do the Learn More. You may want to make overhead transparencies of the Activity Cards and any blackline masters students will be using.

Day 1

Introduce the activity to the class. Begin by discussing each part of the Activity Card:

- The title
- The number of participants (students will most likely be working in pairs)
- Materials (science tools, specimens, books, and other supplies)
- What To Do (directions for completing the activity)
- Boldface words (these are defined in a Glossary in the Teacher's Notes) and any vocabulary unfamiliar to students

- Learn More! (suggestions for extending the activity or for doing further research)
- Pencil icon (a writing prompt). Note that all students should bring paper and pencil with them to the center.

Show students any science equipment, specimens, books, or other materials they will be using in the activity. Have students name the items. Tell students the names of unfamiliar objects and have them repeat the words aloud. Give students a chance to look at the materials and to touch them, if possible. Demonstrate the use of tools and the handling of specimens. Let students know whether they are to do the Learn More. Tell students how you want them to clean up or "reset" the activity when they are done. Typically, they will put the materials where they found them, disassemble any constructions they made (other than artwork), discard any waste, and wipe off the table.

Elicit prior knowledge about the topic from students as appropriate before you begin. Then read the activity aloud, explain any unfamiliar vocabulary, and model, step by step, how to do it, but DO NOT ACTUALLY DO THE ACTIVITY. Instead say, "First I will …. Then I will do … as it says in Step 2 (and so on)." Pantomime certain steps, if necessary. If the activity is a game, arrange for a student volunteer to help you demonstrate how to play it. The idea is to give students a clear picture of what they are to do but without revealing any outcomes or suggesting any conclusions. Tell students that their job will be to discover what happens. When you are finished, show students how to clean up and reset the activity for the next pair of students.

Finally, lead a discussion to help students visualize working at the center.

Ask: What will be the same when you go to the center and do this activity? Elicit that the activity will be done the same way you have just demonstrated.

Ask: What will be different when you go to the center and do this activity? Elicit that each pair of students will do the activity, manipulate the materials, discuss what they are doing, and record their answers. Student pairs will need to work together and help each other.

Day 2

Introduce the second CenterStage Science or other activity that you have chosen for the week. Follow the same procedure as for Day 1.

Day 3

Introduce the third activity that you have chosen for the week. Follow the same procedure as for Day 1.

Day 4

Today you will have a pair of students model working at a center while the rest of the class observes and notes appropriate center procedures and behaviors. Choose a pair of capable students to demonstrate. They should model the procedure (as you did) but not actually do the activity.

Before students leave their seats, review with them how to use the rotation chart. Then have the pair you have chosen model how to think about (out loud for this purpose) where they are going, how they will get there, and what they will do first.

At the established signal, have the pair of students go to the center. Then instruct the rest of the class to quietly gather around them and observe. As the pair gets ready to work, and then reads through and explains each step of the activity, guide the rest of the class in observing those behaviors that are important to successful learning in centers.

You might use questions such as these:

- Did you see how quietly they walked to the learning center?
- Do you see how they are sharing the materials?
- Do you see how they are taking turns reading the directions, writing, and drawing?
- Did you notice that when Sarah forgot what to do, she asked Seth, and he reread the directions for her?
- Did you notice how Sarah set the timer and reminded Seth that it was time to finish up?
- Did you notice what a good job they did of replacing the materials and cleaning up? Did you see how he collected their scrap paper?
- Did you notice how Seth put their completed papers in the folder?
- Did you notice how they pushed in their chairs and went quietly back to their seats?

Now have the student demonstrators share their experience with the class. Ask questions like these:

- What did you like about working in the center?
- How was it different from doing the activity as a whole class?
- What did you do well?
- What did you forget to do?
- How could you make things better the next time you work in a center?

(Repeat this for other centers, but perhaps not in as much detail.)

Day 5

Day 5 is Centers Day! Today all of your careful planning, preparation, and modeling come together.

1. Help students get oriented and stay organized.

   Begin by drawing the students' attention to the grouping chart and rotation plan. (See pages 24 and 25.) Review what the charts show.

   While students are still in their seats, point out the locations of the various centers. Also explain what students who are not working in centers will be doing, e.g., working in small groups with the teacher or an aide, reading independently, playing a game, etc.

   Say: If you are in the Green Leaf pair (for example), please raise your hand.

   Then indicate the center where the pair should go. If students need more reinforcement, tell them to point to the appropriate center as you ask, "If I am in the Green Leaf pair, where should I go?"

2. After students have identified the location of their centers, give the signal that indicates that it is time to move. Have students go to their assigned centers one pair at a time.

   Say: "I see that the Green Leaf pair is ready to move. Please move to your center now."

   Repeat the directions for each group, verbally reinforcing behaviors you expect students to demonstrate during center time.

3. Remind students to set the timers (or notice the time on the clock) at the centers where they will be working. This will remind them when it's time to finish, clean up, and move back to their seats.

At the end of the session, take time to discuss the experience with your students. As students get accustomed to Centers Day or Centers Time, you will not need to debrief them regarding behavior and management after each session. However, discussing the activities themselves will still be very important.

Use the **Class Record Form** to help you keep a record of the activities each student has completed. The forms, which are organized by grade level and subject, can be found in the Blackline Masters section of this *Guide*.

Cleaning Up and Storing Materials

Explain to students that cleaning up will consist of wiping the surface of the work station clean, putting materials back where they found them (or where they are to be stored), and throwing away all waste materials. Provide students with paper towels or other cleaning materials and a container for waste. Students should leave materials in good order for the next group. Specific instructions are provided in the Teacher's Notes as necessary.

After all students have completed a center activity, you or designated students will return the materials to their storage pouches. If you have collected any local materials, you may wish to store them with the corresponding module. In general, any constructions other than artwork (gear assemblies, etc.) should be disassembled and the materials returned to their plastic pouches. Magnets should be stored with their keepers, and batteries removed from their holders. For long-term storage, all materials should be placed in a cool, dry place.

Assessing and Evaluating Learning

"When students are engaged in assessment tasks that are similar in form to tasks in which they will engage in their lives outside the classroom or are similar to the activities of scientists, great confidence can be attached to the data collected. Such assessment tasks are authentic." [*NSES*, p. 83]

Day-to-day assessment—gathering and interpreting information on student learning—is an integral part of teaching. Assessment can reveal a student's academic strengths, weaknesses, and even attitudes. Information gathered through assessment can be used to plan and improve instruction.

Closely related to assessment is evaluation. When educators attach values to information or make judgments about student progress, they are evaluating. Teachers evaluate students in order to develop grading systems, assign grades, and determine whether or not students have mastered a topic.

To assess and evaluate student work in centers, you might use informal assessments, anecdotal records, student work, or student self-evaluations. Each of these is discussed below.

Informal Assessment

Whenever you involve students in a discussion or question-and-answer session, you are conducting an informal assessment. From the responses you get, you begin to form an idea of what your students know about the topic under study. From there, you can decide whether you should reteach the material, provide more examples, or move on to the next topic. When you mark a student's learning dispositions, such as persistence, enthusiasm, courtesy, or effort, you are making judgments based on your informal observations.

As children work in centers, you can document your observations, set goals for individual students, and communicate with students and their families the progress made toward those goals. You may make notes as you observe students working and as you check their completed work.

Informal Assessment Form Date: October 20

Observing and Communicating Skills

Edward	Life Science	Draws careful sketches. Labels even more than asked for. Writes full descriptions using appropriate science vocabulary and noting details.
Mai Li	Life Science	Makes detailed sketches with true colors. Seems proud of art ability. Learning English, but can use many new pertinent words orally. Often asks partner for help with spelling.
William	Life Science	Needs encouragement to draw carefully; wants to finish early. Reads well and can explain to partner.
Glenda	Life Science	Seeks extra reading material. Very quiet; lets partner take lead. Hesitant to draw; be sure partner lets her take turns.
Kenny	Life Science	Has some trouble reading directions, but remembers verbal explanations. Draws well; sometimes forgets to label.

Anecdotal Records

Anecdotal records—narrative notes on individual students—provide a valuable assessment and evaluation tool. Here you can record what students are able to do in the context of what they need to learn next. Anecdotal records provide valuable information to students and families about an individual's strengths that can be used as a foundation for future learning.

You can use the **Individual Anecdotal Record Form** in the Blackline Masters section to make notes about each individual student's work. As you see progress, note it on the form. You will want to be specific in your comments and be sure to note positive behaviors and good work. You might also note how students are making progress toward goals.

Individual Anecdotal Record Form

Kenny B.

Goals:	Increase ability to focus, minimize distracting behaviors, improve reading and writing skills
March 5	Reminded Kenny privately that he must work quietly in centers. Assigned him Amy (a good reader) as a partner. Showed Kenny the Activity Card again during a few minutes of recess and reviewed a few words. Kenny did work more quietly in the center, perhaps because he already knew the vocabulary.
March 12	Talked again with Kenny about quiet behavior and making the center report very legible. He is working on neater curved letters (S, P, C, B, D), so took a sheet of letters with him. Amy agreed to have him write the first part of the report—and his work has slightly improved—a bit neater. Amy reads the directions, and then Kenny rereads them—he finds this helpful.
March 19	Talked to both Amy and Kenny about improved quality of recent work; both seemed pleased and promised to keep up the good work. They took turns reading again. Kenny really seemed to focus so he could reread the directions to her! Report was neat with labeled drawings. Perhaps Kenny is seeing that he can do better work when he tries—and when he has a little support!
March 26	Despite spilling (and quietly cleaning up) some soil, Kenny did well in the science center again this week. I had reviewed a few key words with him again. He and Amy now take turns reading and writing. Kenny has set a goal for himself of writing on the lines. Again, more progress in motivation and behavior! Kenny was able to explain how he and Amy classified each kind of soil.

Student Work

Since students are working with a partner in the centers, you may want each pair to complete just one Response Sheet (or one notebook page) for each of the activities. Students can negotiate the particulars as long as the work represents a joint effort. This parallels the work of some scientific research teams, leaves more time for investigation, and eases your workload. Tell students that both of their names should be on any papers they turn in. Of course, you may prefer to have students turn in their own individual work.

Decide on a place near the center for finished work to be placed. Label this turn-in folder or tray clearly and remind students that their last step in completing an activity is to turn in their work.

Suggested answers or guidelines for assessment are given for each activity in the Teacher's Notes for each module. Check student papers to be sure that all questions are addressed and that charts, drawings, and other representations are complete and properly labeled. Determine the value you will place on the use of complete sentences, correct spelling, and proper use of new vocabulary. Communicate this to students. You may wish to use a rubric such as the one shown here.

3 Work is of excellent quality

Includes, as applicable, insightful observations, full descriptions, detailed drawings, complete charts or diagrams, conclusions drawn from data.

2 Work is of acceptable quality

Includes, as applicable, most observations, drawings, charts or diagrams; conclusions are somewhat logical.

1 Work needs improvement

Student needs guidance in making complete, legible answers.

After all pairs of students have completed an activity, or after several activities on related topics have been completed, conduct a class discussion (debriefing) about the activities. Use questions such as these to stimulate conversation and the sharing of ideas: *What did you learn? What surprised you? How could we use this information? How could we explain this to a younger person or to someone who has not done the activity? How did making drawings help you learn or share what you learned? If we used this activity again, how could we extend it? What could we change to make it better?*

Student Self-Evaluation

In order to become self-directed learners, "students need the opportunity to evaluate and reflect on their own scientific understanding and ability." [NSES, p. 88]

Even young students can think about their own work and express their opinions as to how well they have done it. Having students evaluate their own work conveys to them the idea that they are responsible and independent learners.

Use the **Student Self-Evaluation Form** in the Blackline Masters section to help students think about their own work.

Student Self-Evaluation

Name _____

I worked on Activity # ____ in Center ____.

I worked with _____. (classmate's name)

I shared materials.   😊 😐 ☹

I took turns.   😊 😐 ☹

I helped with reading, recording, and drawing.   😊 😐 ☹

I learned _____
_____
_____

I did a good job of _____.

Next time I could improve _____.

CenterStage™ Science Learning Centers

Family and Community Involvement

Educators, families, and the community at large all share responsibility for helping children develop critical thinking skills—skills that are necessary not only for their academic success, but also for success in their everyday lives as adults. Scientifically literate citizens understand the importance of science in their daily lives, can better evaluate public policy decisions, and can make more informed decisions about science-related reports in the media. According to the National Science Education Standards [NRC, 1996], effective elementary school science programs require "access to the world beyond the classroom." [NRC, p. 220]. As you and your students explore the excitement of hands-on, minds-on science using the CenterStage Science modules, consider using real world experiences or field trips either as an introduction to the concepts and process skills involved in your unit of study or as an exciting culminating event.

By developing relationships with local colleges, businesses, and industry, you can help your students gain access to scientists and other professionals. They, in turn, can provide you and your students with invaluable access to their expertise, materials, and equipment. Also consider the many other resources available, such as the school grounds themselves, nature preserves, museums, zoos, or even supermarket garden centers and farm cooperatives. If it is not possible to visit a museum or zoo, consider taking a virtual field trip online. Consider inviting guest speakers into your classroom to enhance your science units. Students will enjoy the interaction, and the experience will help them make the connection between the concept they are learning in class and its application to the real world. Through their interaction with community members, students can better understand local as well as national issues that require a level of scientific literacy: pollution, energy, conservation, health care, meteorology, and so forth. Students may even be inspired to pursue a career in science or in a science-related field.

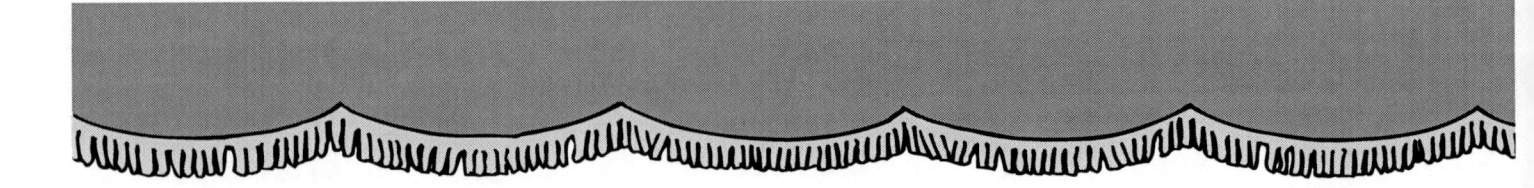

Family involvement is crucial in fostering and supporting a child's curiosity, creativity, and educational success. When your students are working on the CenterStage Science investigations, invite family members to volunteer to help. They may enjoy helping to set up and clear away the materials, keeping students on task, or just listening as the children explain their work. When you encourage family members to become engaged in their child's education through CenterStage Science activities, you help them learn more about the concepts and processes of science for themselves. This will, in turn, help them to more effectively encourage their child's interest in science. Family members may also enjoy sharing science-related interests or hobbies with the class, which will further enrich the school-home connection and the quality of your science program.

Holding a "Family CenterStage Science Night," where your students can lead their family members through CenterStage Science investigations, can stimulate excitement and interest in science for both elementary school children and their families. It can encourage families to become more involved in their child's science education. Research suggests that children with parents who are involved in their education perform at higher levels than children whose parents are not involved. Surveys also indicate that parents pass on to their children their own attitudes toward science—whether positive or negative. Family "science nights" with CenterStage Science modules offer you an opportunity to involve parents and children in a positive science experience.

Wish List

As you use CenterStage Science activities, you will probably think of local or purchased materials you could add, books that would reinforce and extend concepts, and resource people whose expertise would enrich the CenterStage Science experience. Use this space to make notes about these for future reference.

CenterStage™ Science Learning Centers · Teacher's Resource Guide

References

Chessin, D.A., and J.M. Shaw, 2002. *Science Investigations Toolkit: Professional Development Guide for Teachers K–8.* Vernon Hills, Illinois: ETA/Cuisenaire.

Jensen, Eric. 1998. *Teaching with the Brain in Mind.* Alexandria, Virginia: Association for Supervision and Curriculum Development.

National Research Council. 1996. *National Science Education Standards.* Washington, D.C.: National Academy Press.

Tomlinson, Carol Ann. 2002. *The Differentiated Classroom: Responding to the Needs of All Learners.* Alexandria, Virginia: Association for Supervision and Curriculum Development.

Wiggans, G., and J. McTighe. 1998. *Understanding by Design.* Alexandria, Virginia: Association for Supervision and Curriculum Development.

Wiske, M.S., ed. 1998. *Teaching for Understanding.* San Francisco: Jossey Bass.

Blackline Masters

Family and Community Involvement

    Volunteer Sign-In Sheet 42

    Volunteer's Notes 43

    Volunteer Badges 44

    Notes to Families • Visitor's Day 45

    Notes to Families • Call for Volunteers 46

Classroom Management

    Safety Guidelines 47

    Rules for Learning Centers 48

    Student Self-Evaluation 49

    Informal Assessment Form 50

    Individual Anecdotal Record Form 51

    Class Record Forms. 52–60

Volunteer Sign-In Sheet

Thank you for being here!

Name **Date** **Time In** **Time Out**

Volunteer's Notes

My Name _____

Group _____

Students I Worked With	Activity/Skill	Notes and Observations

Volunteer Badges

Thank you for coming! **VISITOR**
My Name Is

Thank you for coming! **VISITOR**
My Name Is

Thank you for coming! **VISITOR**
My Name Is

Thank you for coming! **VISITOR**
My Name Is

Thank you for coming! **VISITOR**
My Name Is

Thank you for coming! **VISITOR**
My Name Is

44 Teacher's Resource Guide CenterStage™ Science Learning Centers

Notes to Families • Visitor's Day

Dear Family,

We are using CenterStage™ Science learning centers as part of our science program. Students work in pairs or individually at different centers once each week for 20 minutes. Our Centers Day is _____.

In three weeks, each student will have had a chance to work in every center. Centers also give me a chance to work with small groups of students more often.

If you would like to visit our classroom and learn more about our science centers, please join us on Visitor's Day!

Date: _____

Time: _____

Sincerely,

P.S. Please cut off the bottom of this form for your child to return.

Check a box, sign, and have your child return this part.

☐ Yes! I/We will come to Visitor's Day!

☐ I/We will not be able to come to Visitor's Day.

Signed: _____

My child's name: _____

Notes to Families • Call for Volunteers

Dear Families,

Have you heard about our CenterStage Science Centers? I hope that your child has shared the news. Science Centers help me give your child individualized attention in science at least one day each week.

It helps our Centers Day a lot when there is an adult available at each center to oversee a small group of students as they work. You don't need to know anything about science. Sometimes the group has a question about the activity card directions. An adult to turn to helps the center run more smoothly.

The schedule below shows the days and times when I have scheduled CenterStage™ Science learning centers. Please write in your name and phone number and a day when you will be available. I will then call you to confirm. Thank you.

Sincerely,

Science Centers Volunteer Sign-Up Sheet

Day and Date	Time	Your Name and Number
_____	_____	_____
		Telephone
_____	_____	_____
		Telephone
_____	_____	_____
		Telephone
_____	_____	_____
		Telephone

Safety Guidelines

- Do not taste, eat, or drink any materials.
- Wash your hands after handling messy materials.
- Report any accidents.
- Tell your teacher if you have allergies or other medical problems.
- Wear safety goggles.

Rules for Learning Centers

1. Respect yourself and others.
2. Follow directions.
3. Use quiet voices.
4. Take turns.
5. Share the materials and share the work.
6. Manage your time.
7. Clean up before you leave.

Student Self-Evaluation

Name _____

I worked on Activity # _____ **in Center** _____.

I worked with _____. (classmate's name)

I shared materials.   😊 😐 ☹

I took turns.   😊 😐 ☹

I helped with reading, recording, and drawing.   😊 😐 ☹

I learned _____
_____
_____

I did a good job of _____.

Next time I could improve _____.

Informal Assessment Form Date: _____

Learning Goal _____

Group _____ **Center** _____

Student	Activities Completed	Notes and Observations

Individual Anecdotal Record Form

Student's Name _____

Date   **Observations**

Class Record Form: Grade 1 Physical Science

Name	1. Soak It Up!	2. Float or Sink?	3. Compare and Weigh	4. Think and Sort	5. How Does It Change?	6. The Spring Toy	7. Dizzy Dinosaurs	8. The Dino-Go-Round	9. What's That Sound?	10. How Light Travels	11. New Colors	12. Does Light Shine Through?	13. We Use Electricity	14. Static Electricity	15. Pick It Up	16. Magnet Puppets	17. How Many Paper Clips?	18. The Position Game	Notes

Class Record Form: Grade 1 Life Science

Name	1 All Kinds of Mammals	2 Hide-and-Seek Dominoes	3 What's Inside Me?	4 Terrific Teeth	5 The Otter Skull	6 A Closer Look at Teeth	7 Fruits and Vegetables	8 Is It an Insect?	9 Good Senses	10 Seeds to Sort	11 What's Inside a Seed?	12 Animal Babies	13 Plant a Seed	14 Vegetable or Fruit?	15 Eggs to Chickens	16 Trick, Hide, and Scare	17 Sea Dragons	18 The Rabbit and the Hedgehog	Notes

CenterStage™ Science Learning Centers — Teacher's Resource Guide — 53

© ETA/Cuisenaire

Class Record Form: Grade 1 Earth Science

Name	1. The Water Cycle	2. All Kinds of Rocks	3. Sort the Rocks	4. Earth Materials	5. Recycle It	6. Water, Water, Everywhere	7. What Soil Feels Like	8. Colorful Soils	9. Look at Fossils	10. Fossils and Shells	11. Shark's Teeth	12. Earth and the Sun	13. Up in the Sky	14. Different Seasons	15. Making Shadows	16. Cloud Shapes	17. Day and Night	18. Our Helpful Sun	Notes

54 Teacher's Resource Guide CenterStage™ Science Learning Centers

© ETA/Cuisenaire

Class Record Form: Grade 2 Physical Science

Name	1 Sorting Buttons	2 Weigh to Go	3 Liquids and Solids	4 Lifting with Levers	5 Pendulum	6 Ramp It Up	7 Wheels and Axles	8 Twist and Turn	9 The Vibrating Ruler	10 The Cup Phone	11 Reflecting Light	12 Magnify with Water	13 Light Up the Bulb	14 Conductors	15 Attract or Repel?	16 What Do Magnets Attract?	17 Which Magnet is Stronger?	18 Mystery Object Game	Notes

CenterStage™ Science Learning Centers — Teacher's Resource Guide

Class Record Form: Grade 2 Life Science

Name	1 Snails and Slugs	2 Dinosaurs	3 Mealworm Life Cycle	4 All Kinds of Sea Stars	5 A Close Look at Sea Stars	6 Insect Models	7 Insect—or Not?	8 Mammal, Reptile, or Amphibian?	9 Meet the Mealworm	10 Looking at Leaves	11 Vein Patterns in Leaves	12 Eye See	13 Reptiles	14 Our Special Traits	15 A Closer Look at Mealworms	16 We Need Trees	17 Animal Homes	18 Animal Tic-Tac-Toe	Notes

56 Teacher's Resource Guide CenterStage™ Science Learning Centers

© ETA/Cuisenaire

Class Record Form: Grade 2 Earth Science

Name	1. Liquids and Solids	2. Sorting Rocks	3. Odd One Out	4. Comparing Rocks	5. Weathering Rocks	6. Rocks and Sand	7. Soil Art	8. Dino Tracks	9. Fossils	10. A Rocky Path	11. A Fault Line	12. Volcanic Rocks	13. Humidity	14. Static Attraction	15. Sun and Shadows	16. Lunar Trip	17. The Nine Planets	18. Planet Matching	Notes

CenterStage™ Science Learning Centers — Teacher's Resource Guide

Class Record Form: Grade 3 Physical Science

Name	1. What Is Its Mass?	2. Property Mysteries	3. Solid, Liquid, or Gas?	4. Carry the Load	5. Building Bridges	6. Make It Strong	7. The Mighty Lever	8. Up the Ramp	9. Pulley It Up	10. Gears Here	11. Gears at Work	12. Attract Through Solids	13. Make a Circuit	14. Add a Switch	15. Two Kinds of Circuits	16. Taking the Temperature	17. Use a Tuning Fork	18. Reflect on Your Name	Notes

58 Teacher's Resource Guide   CenterStage™ Science Learning Centers

Class Record Form: Grade 3 Life Science

Name	1 Insects Up Close	2 The Wasp and the Fly	3 What Do Spiders Eat?	4 Cool Worms	5 Study and Sort	6 Desert Plants	7 Desert Animals	8 Predators	9 Animal Match	10 Tree Cookies	11 Tree Ring Clues	12 Our Important Lungs	13 Breathing Rate	14 The Beat Goes On	15 The Stomach	16 Eye to Eye	17 Fingerprint Hints	18 Ruler Reaction Time	Notes

CenterStage™ Science Learning Centers — Teacher's Resource Guide — 59

© ETA/Cuisenaire

Class Record Form: Grade 3 Earth Science

Name	1. What Mineral is it?	2. Sorting Minerals	3. Streak Test	4. All About Soil	5. Soil Sample	6. Water and Soil	7. Testing Textures	8. Preventing Erosion	9. A Careful Look at Fossils	10. Sorting Fossils	11. Trilobites	12. Learning with Planet Cards	13. Solar System Model	14. Volcanic Mechanics	15. Quakes and Shakes	16. Types of Clouds	17. Weather the Storm	18. A Planet Card Game	Notes